MOTIVATIONAL DOODLES
adult coloring book

STAY FOCUSED

Misty McDivitt

19 detailed kaleidodoodles

Hillbilly Art
5333 Fort Henry Drive
Kingsport, TN 37663
www.facebook.com/hillbillyartcoloringbooks
hillbillyart77@outlook.com

Printed in the United States of America

this book
belongs
to

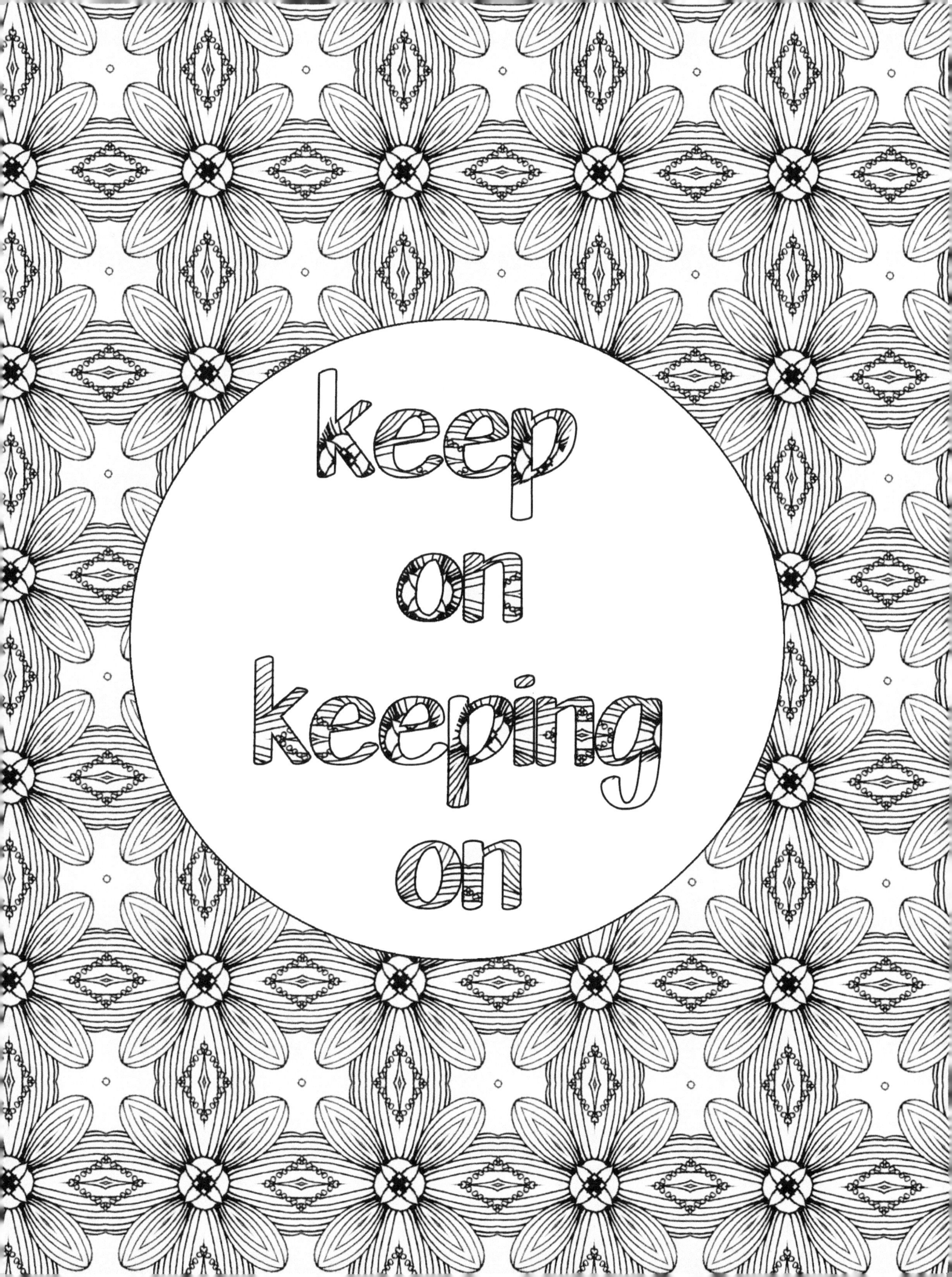

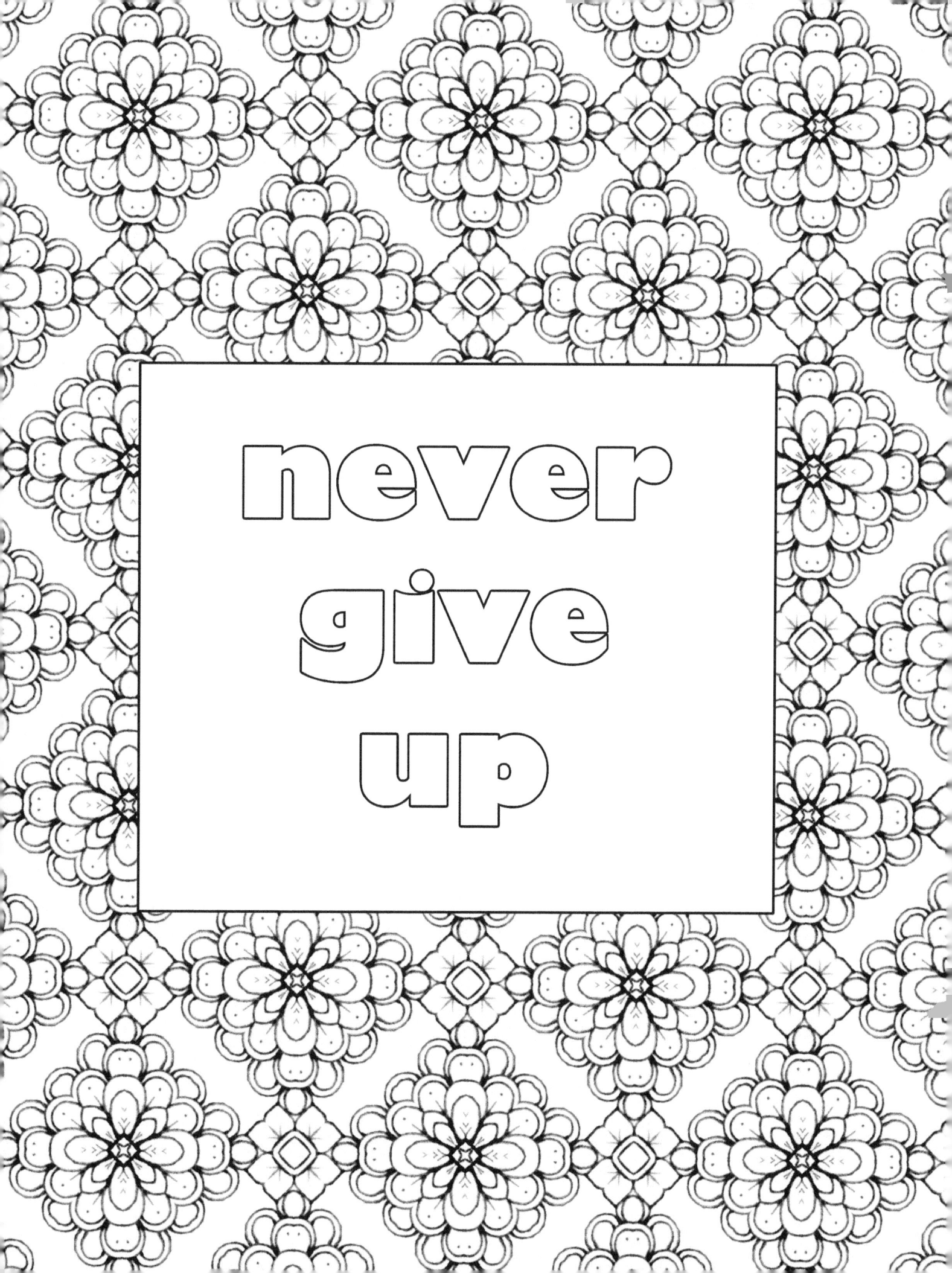

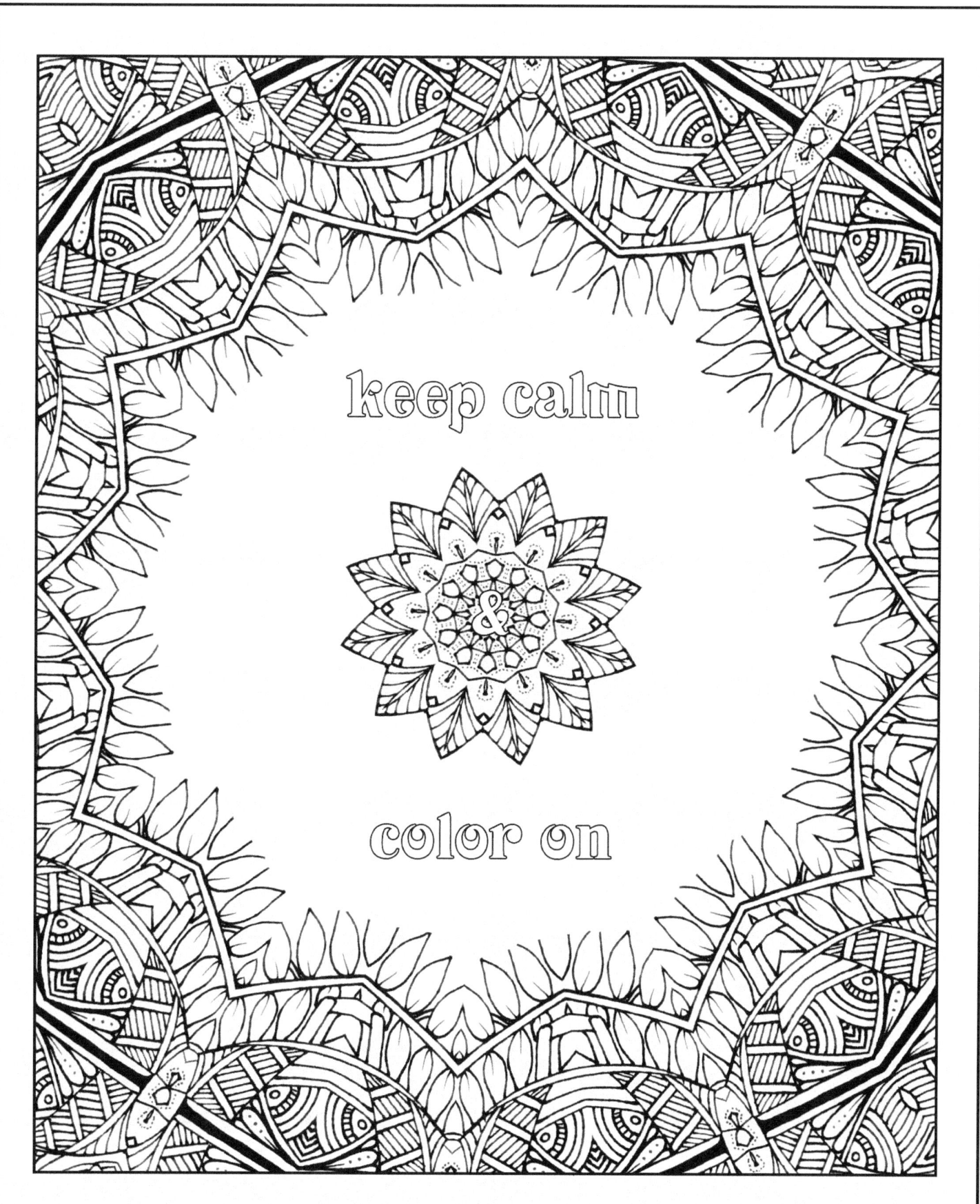

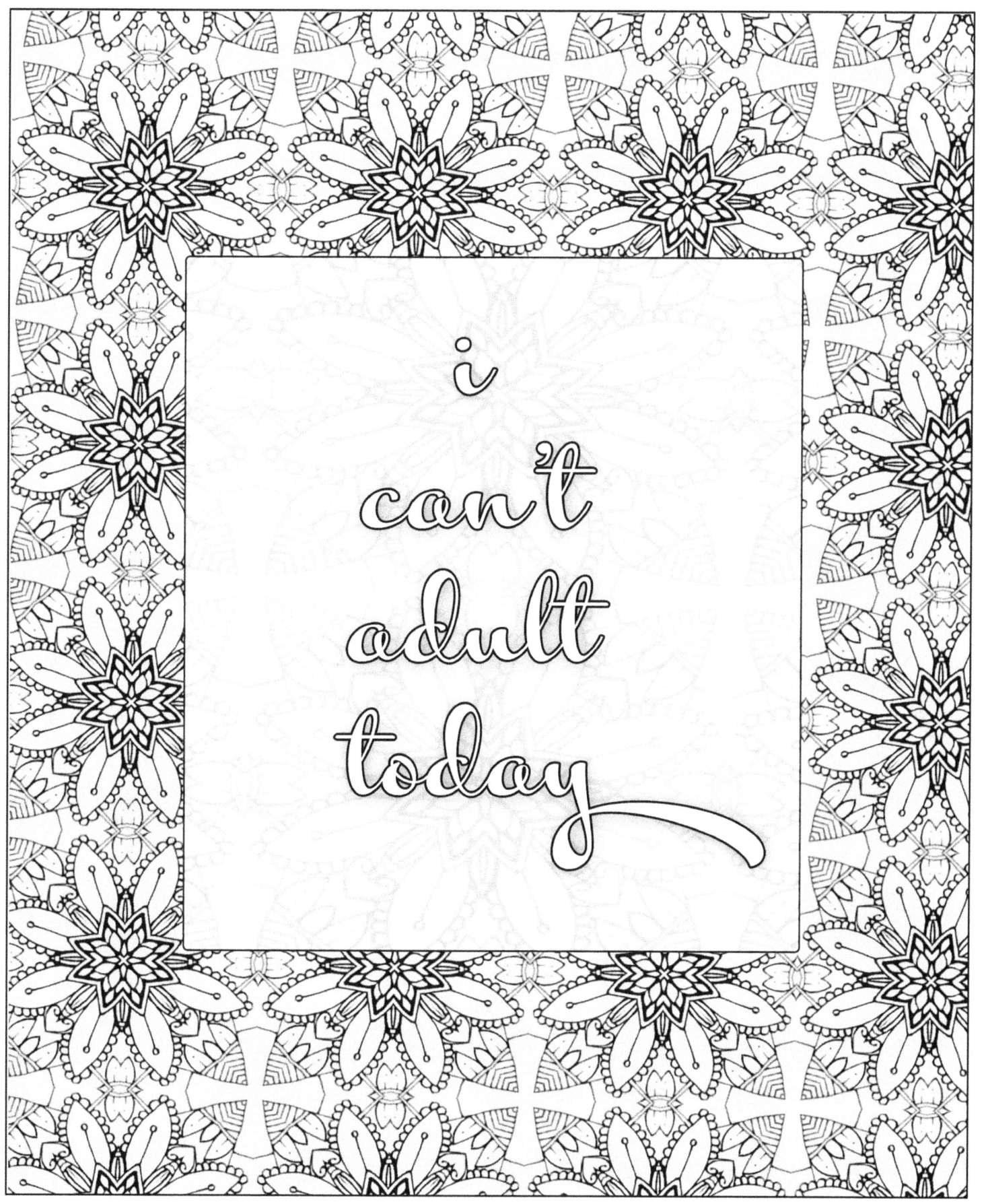

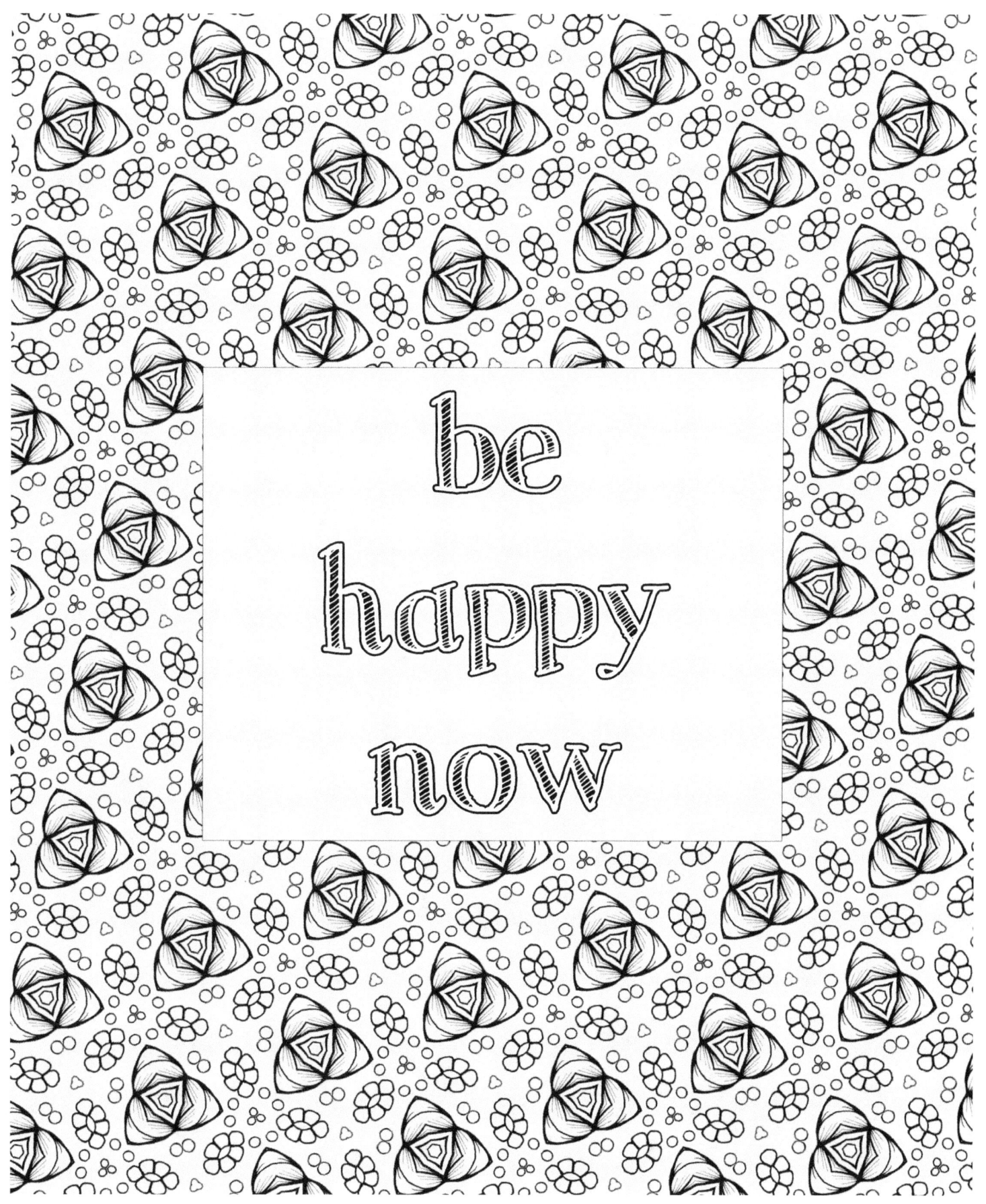

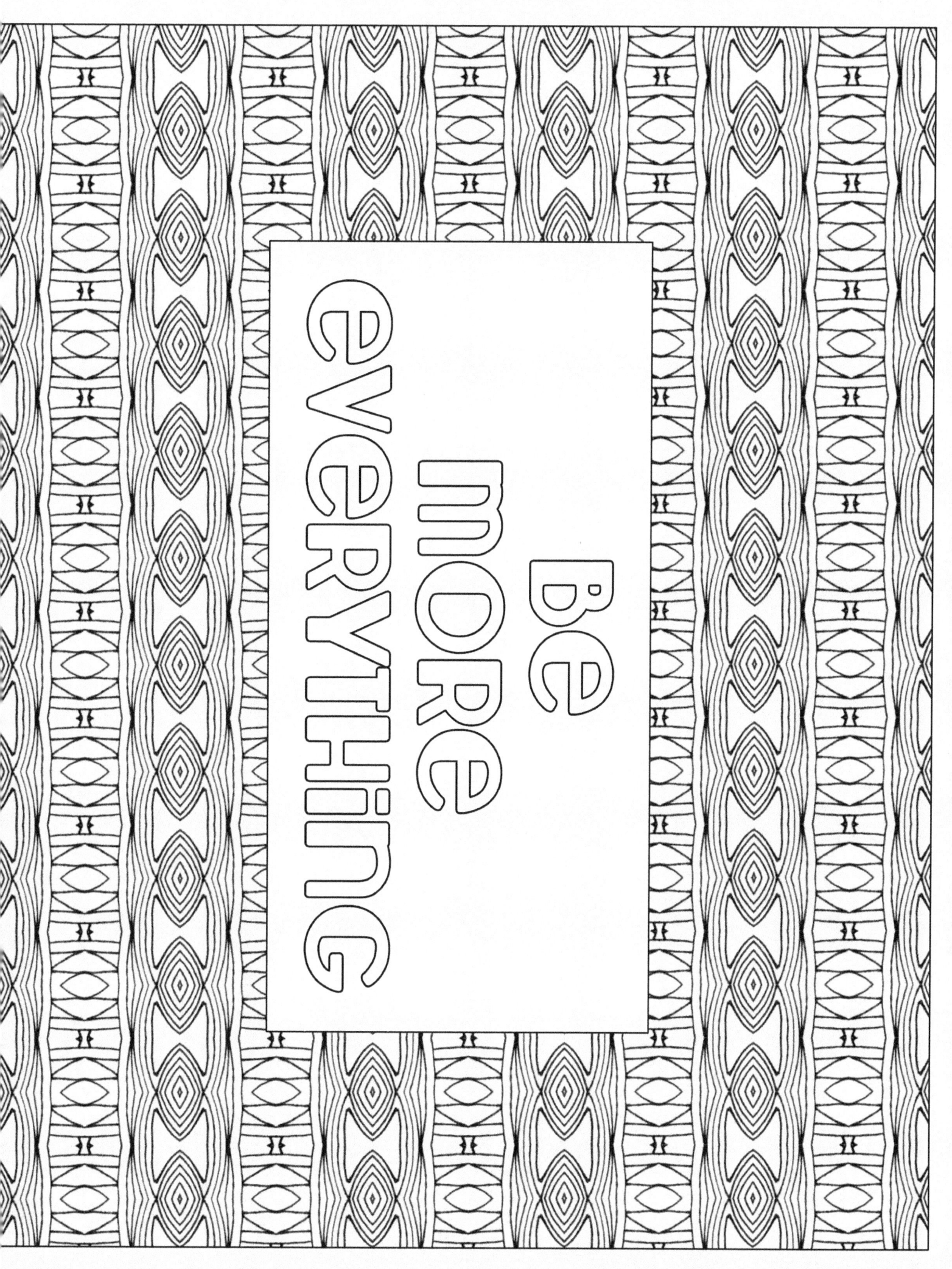

Be
moRe
everything

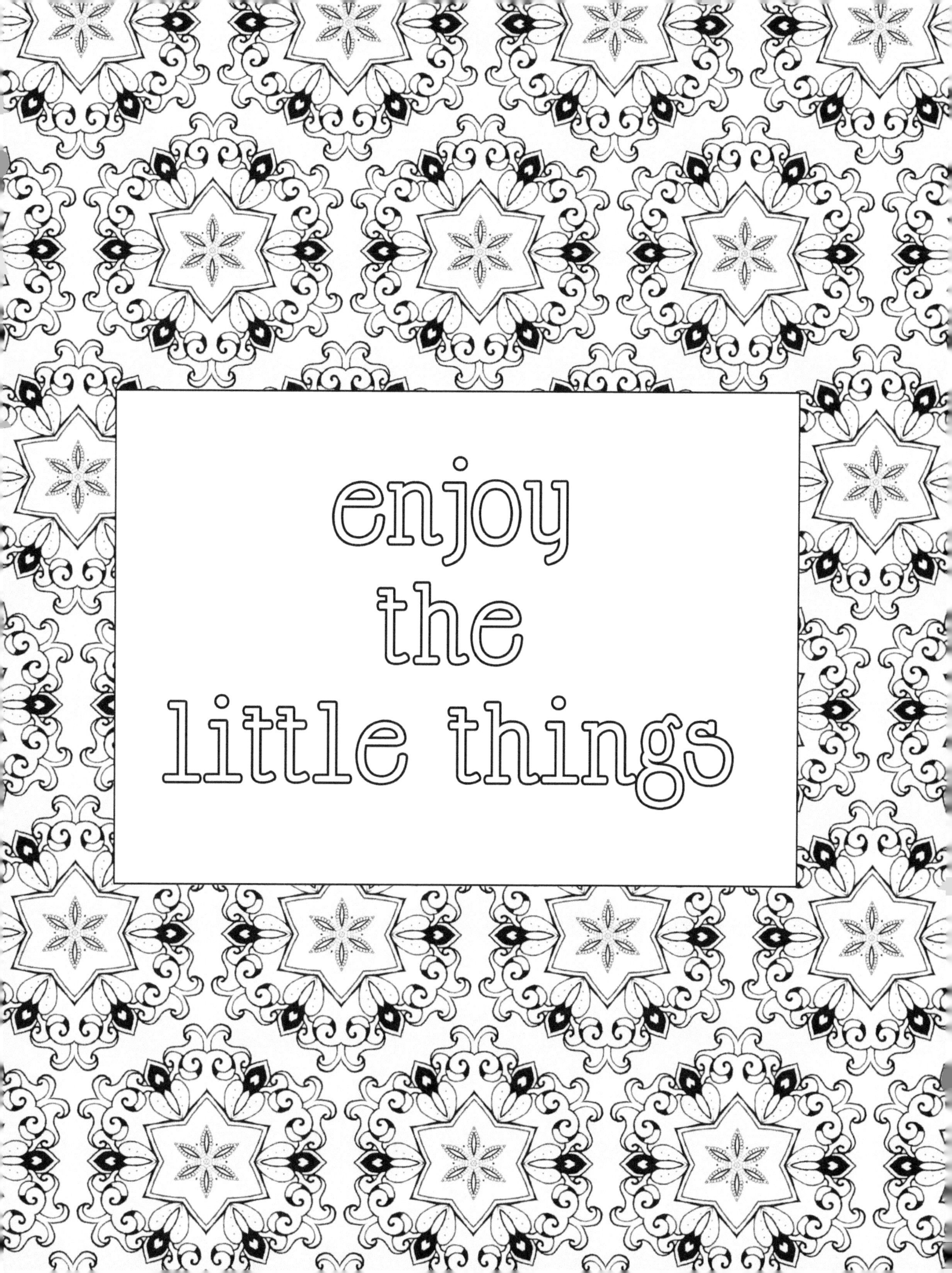

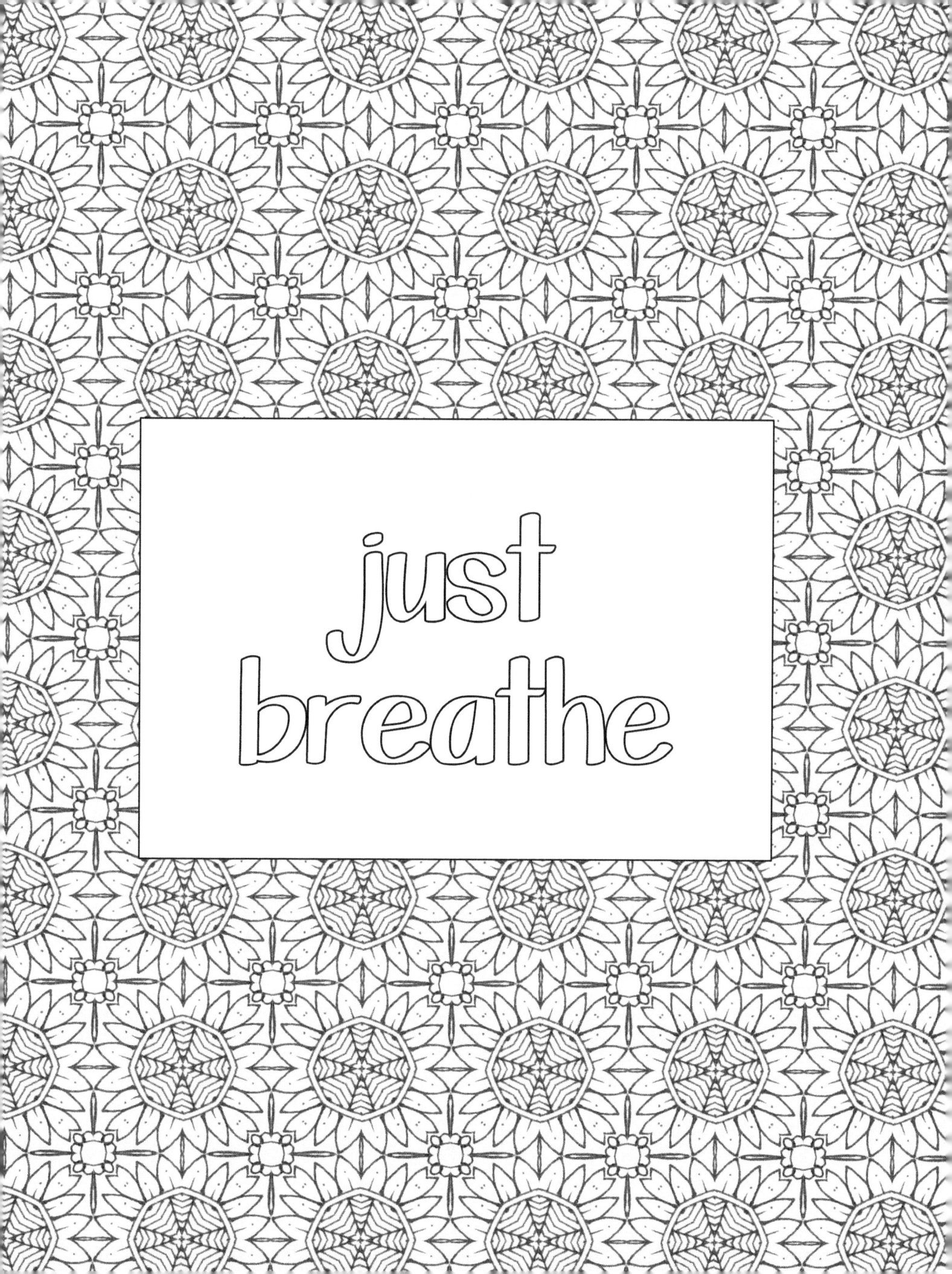

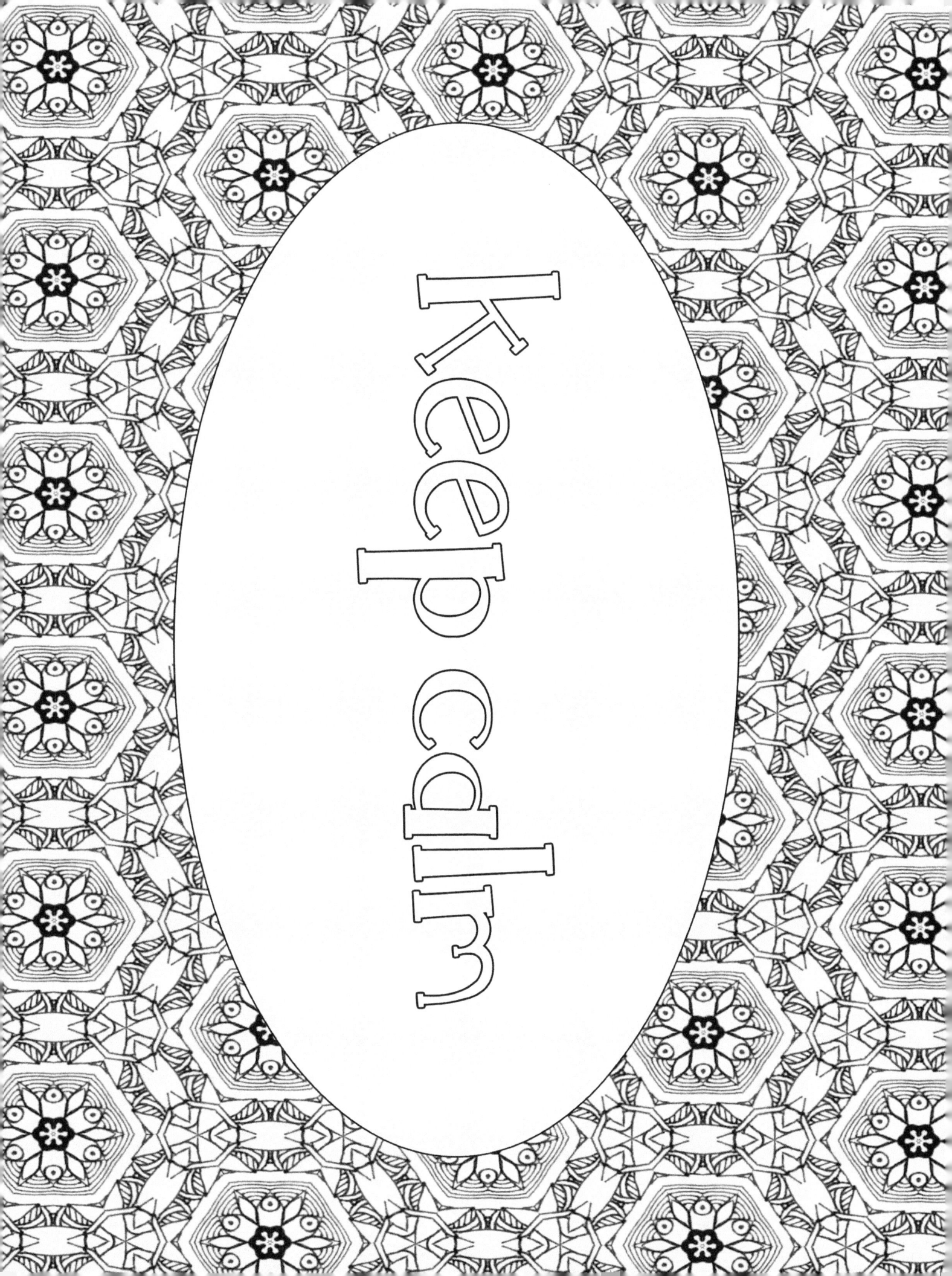

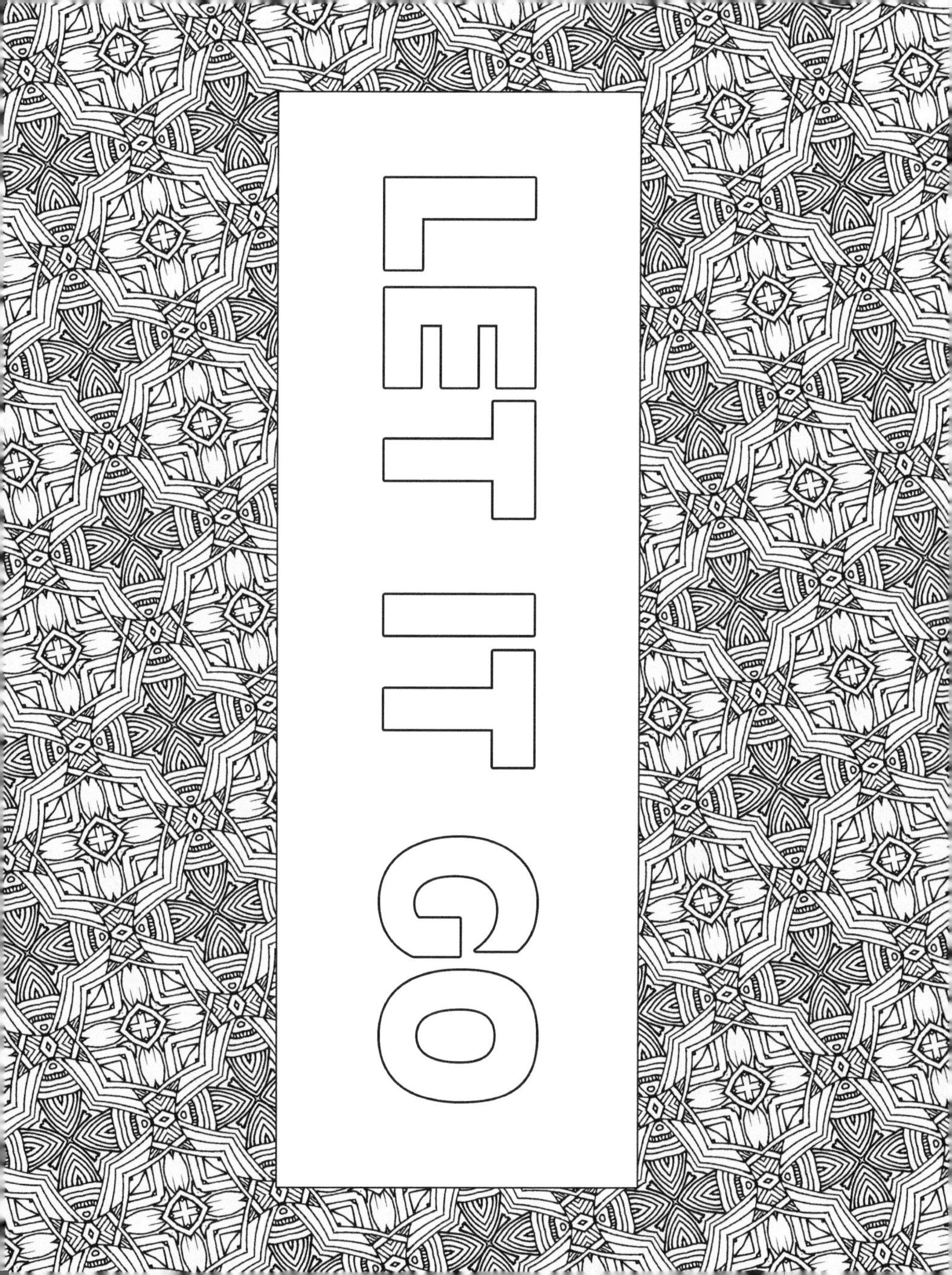

LET IT GO

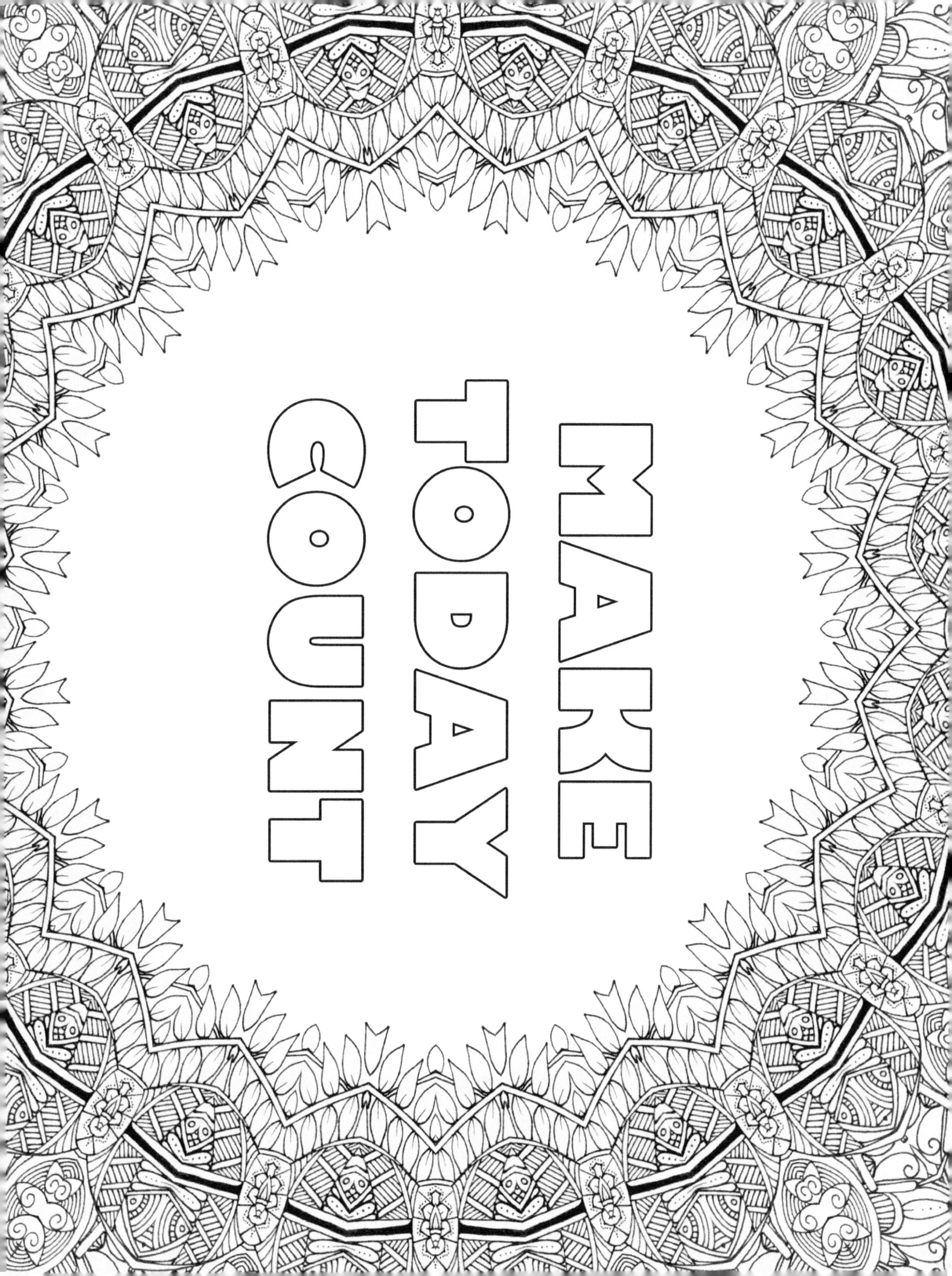

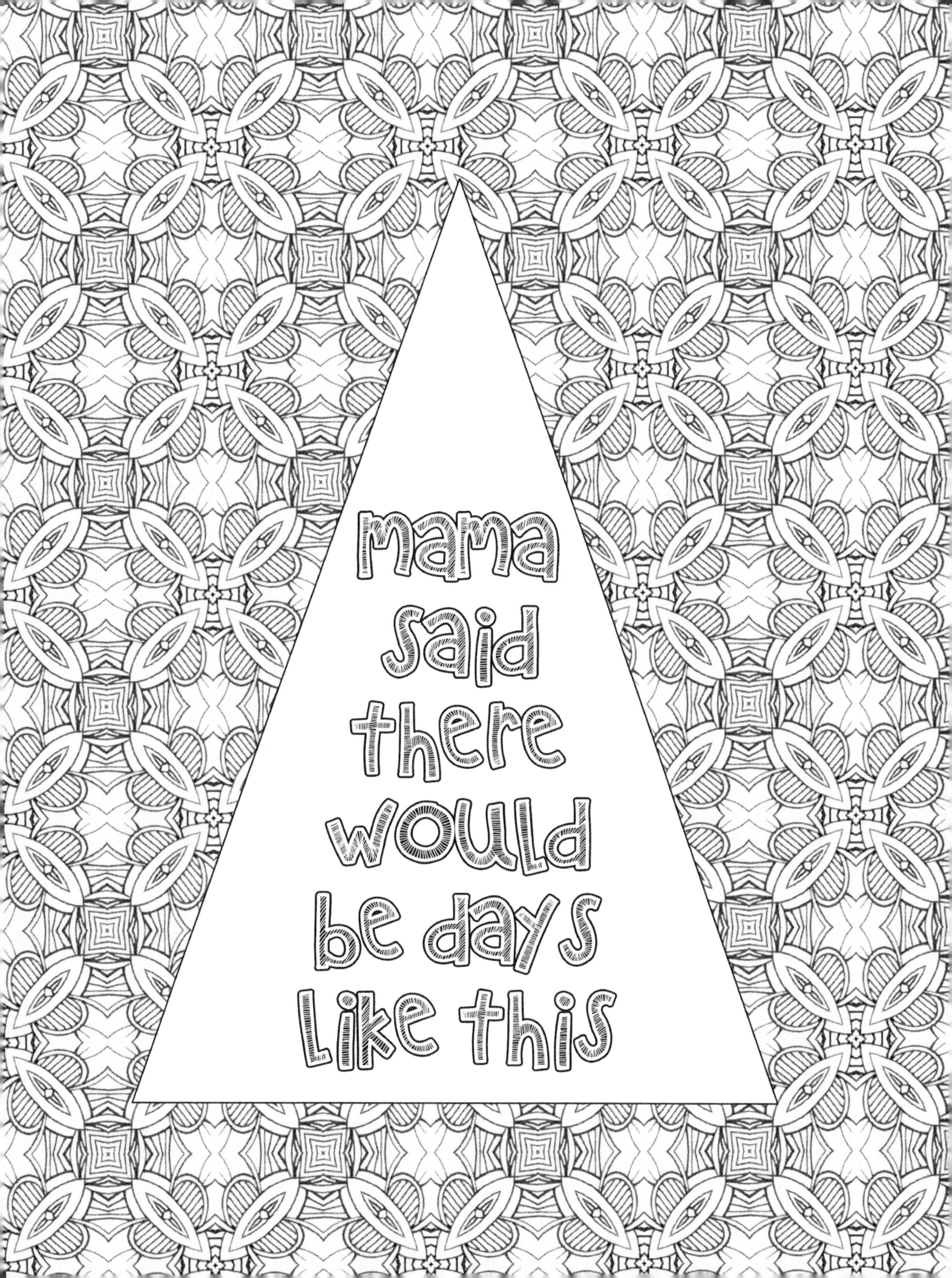

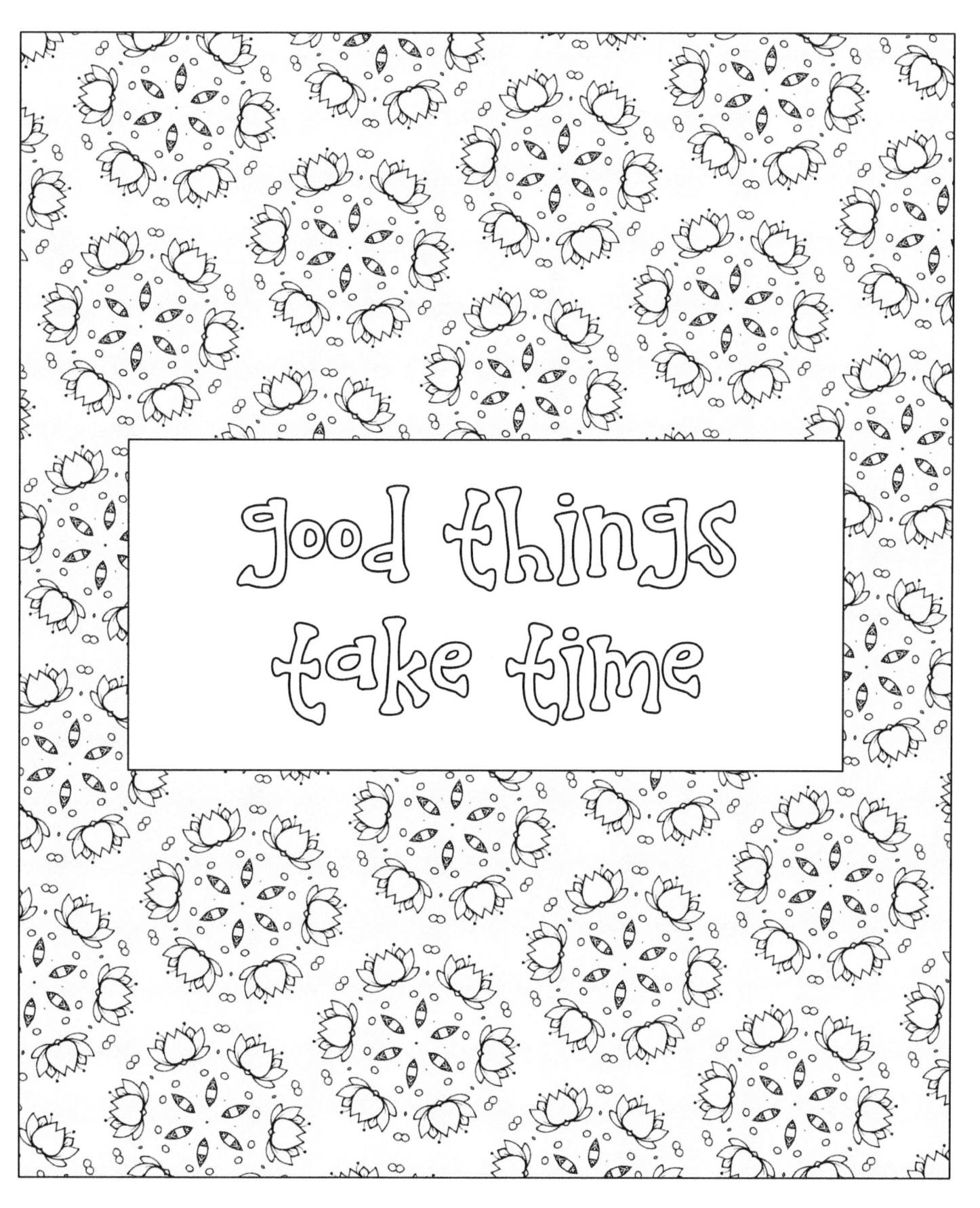

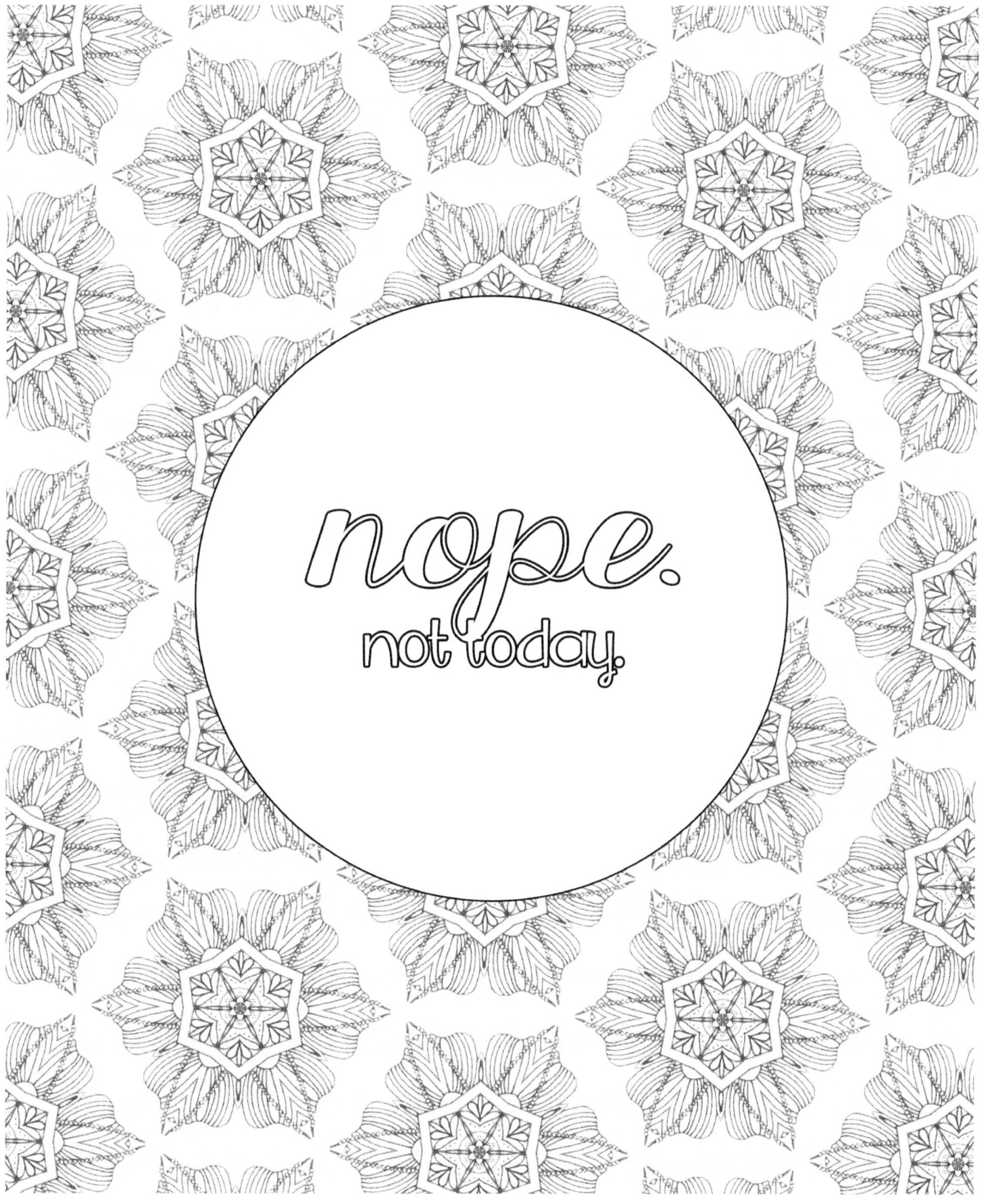

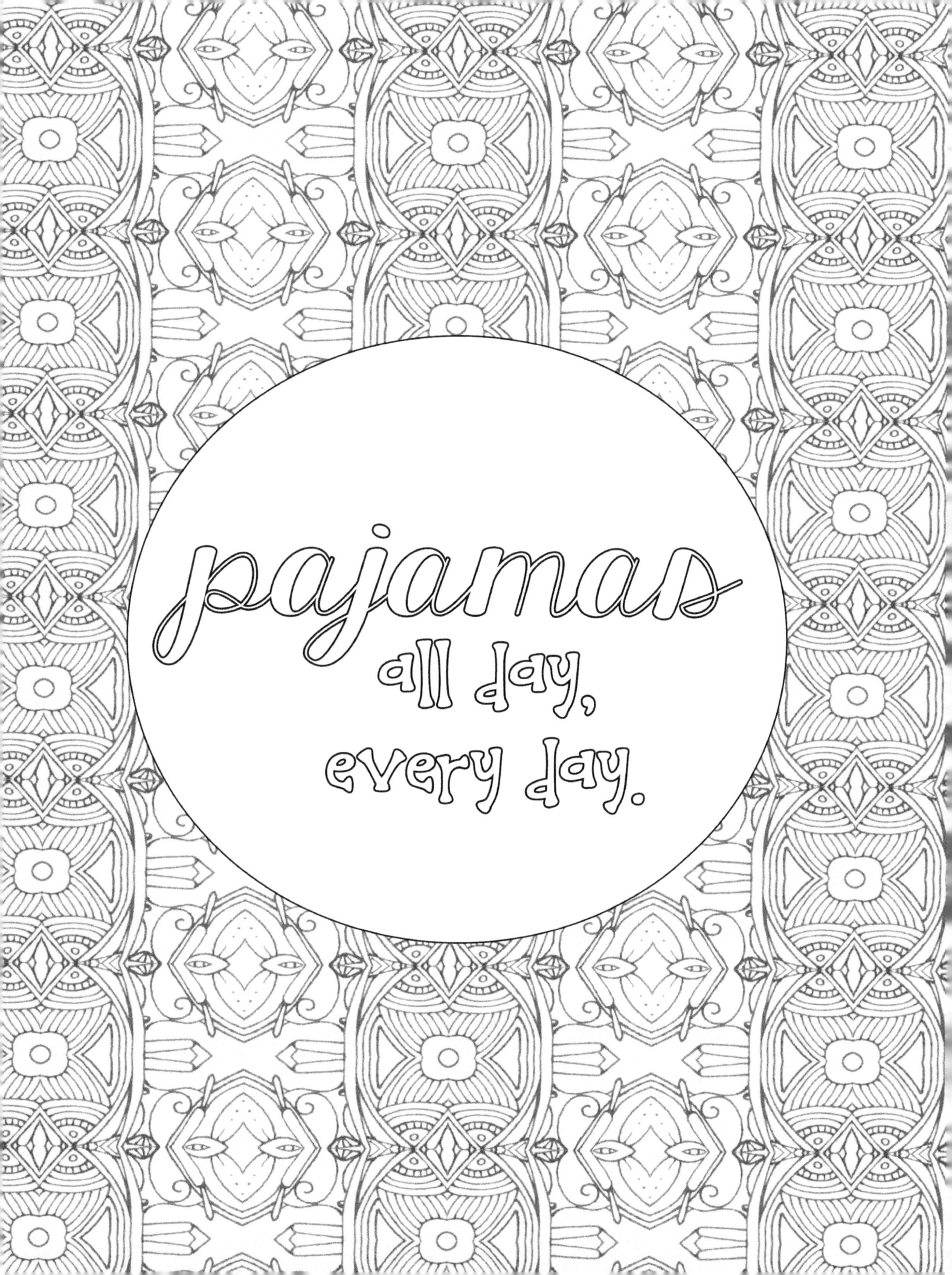

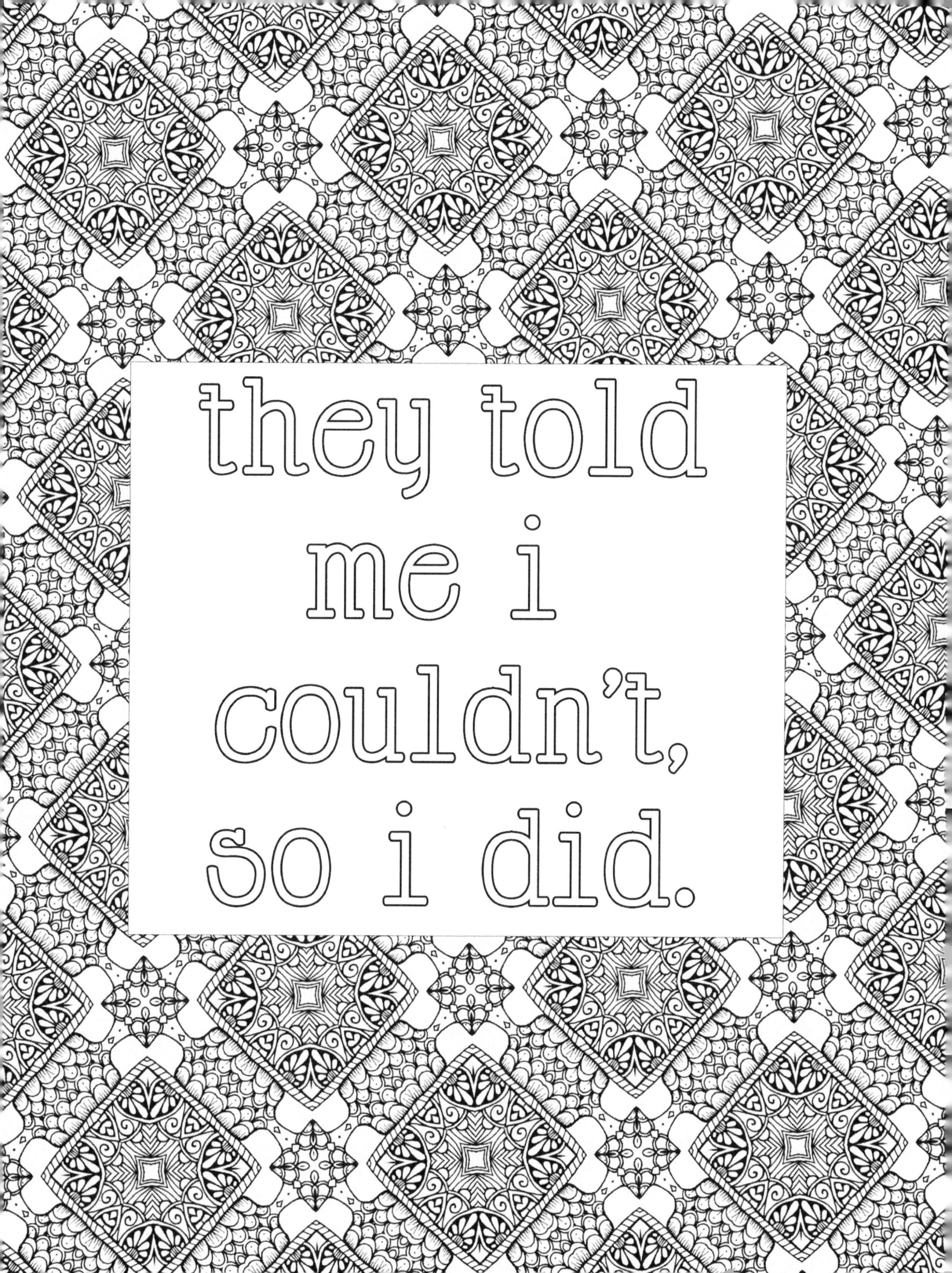

they told me i couldn't, so i did.

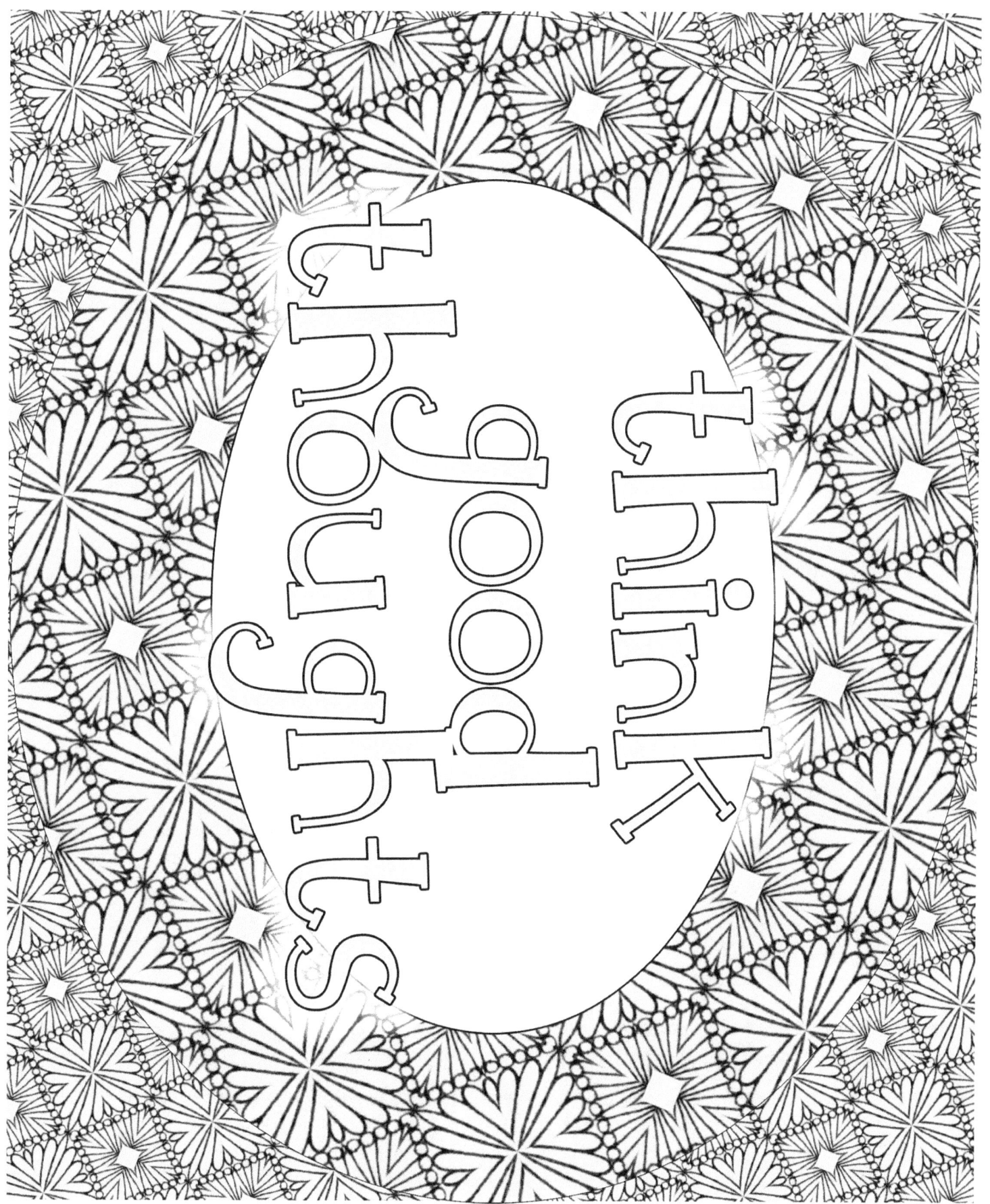

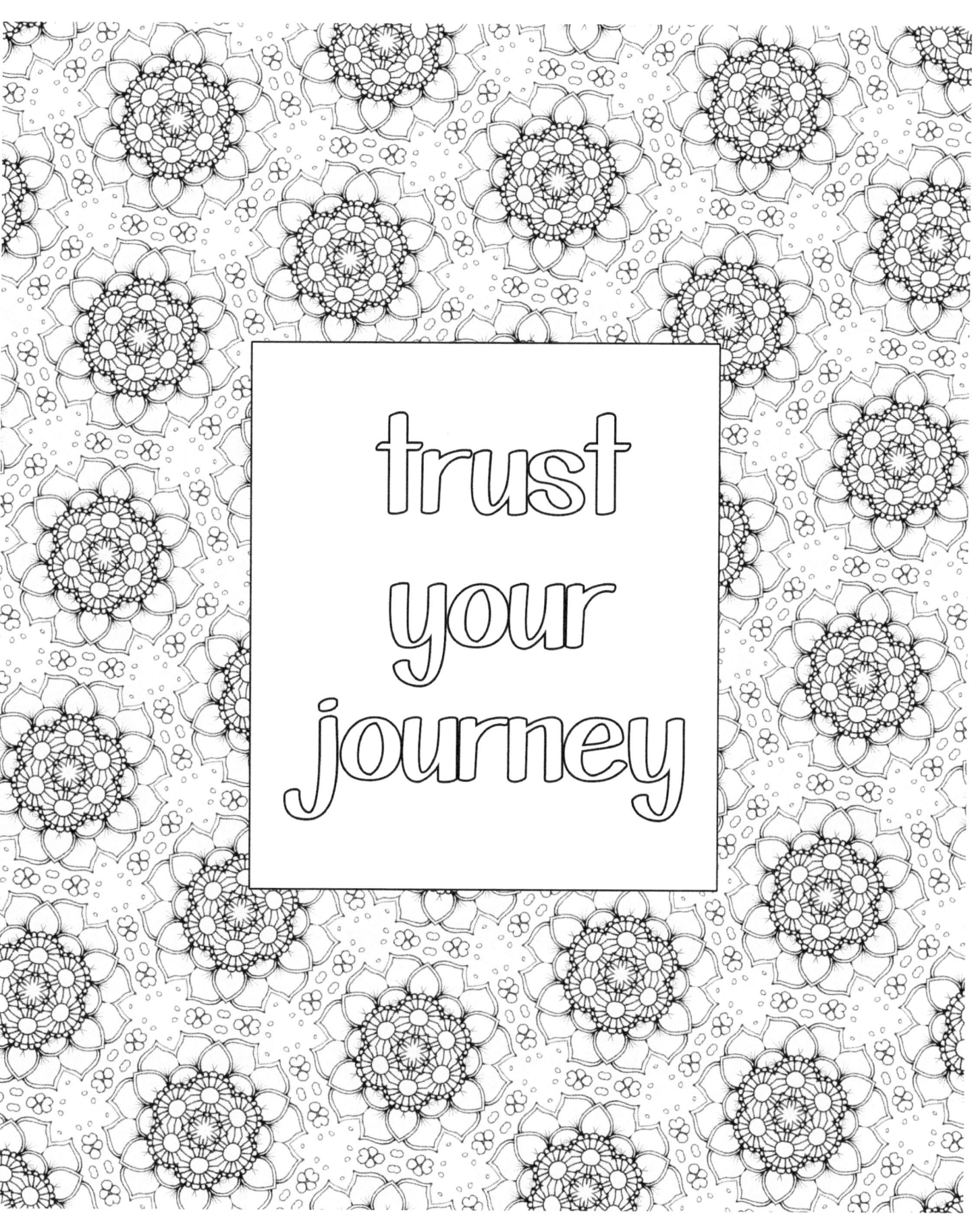